MW01104105

THE PROOF
IS IN THE PUDDING!

_____ *a pocket book of hope* _____

*A collection of inspirational true
stories of mystical events in the
Spiritual Reality of people's lives and
quotes and poems of inspiration.*

Doug Zeigler

Produced by:

FriesenPress

Suite 300 – 852 Fort Street
Victoria, BC, Canada V8W 1H8

www.friesenpress.com

Distributed to the trade by The Ingram Book Company

Table of Contents

ACKNOWLEDGEMENTS

I WOULD LIKE TO THANK MY WIFE ANN, SISTERS Darlene, Sheila, Shirley, my brothers Charles, Allen and my mother Katherine, for their love throughout my life. A special thanks to my grandmother Beatrice, who helped me in my darkest hour, when my need was the greatest and of course her unconditional love; and to the friends and family who provided their stories for my book: Richard, John, Phil, Nettie, Shelley and Gerri.

I cannot leave out Plotinus, who kept me informed throughout my writing of the wonderful stories of the invisible reality and by his personal out body unions with the 'One' or the Absolute Source to Creation.

The Hummingbird carving on the front cover was done by my brother Charles Batt, 1943-2009. He lived in Victoria BC. Charles give his little carved birds as a act of kindness to passerby`s in James Bay of Victoria. Which give the giver much joy!

Message to my Readers:

Listen to your human spirit and everything will fall into place. 'The Veil is there, just open the door and visit paradise.' For the skeptics, please take this advice:

"There is a principle which is a bar against all information, which is proof against all arguments and which cannot fail to keep a man in everlasting igno-rance...that principle is contempt prior to investigation."

—*William Paley (1743-1805)*

Keep an open mind and be silent to hear the voice within, which is your Soul, and then follow your destiny. Yes it is true we have advanced in technology and science, however it seems as if Dr. Eben Alexander is correct, it does not compare to the spiritual reality. His experience tells us from his book, Proof of Heaven "we have nothing to fear and Om loves us." Proof is in the Pudding, means that to fully test something you need to experience it yourself. Because I have experienced this reality like many others have, I like to point this out, to bring hope and help make a better world.

Love & Peace, Doug

Hope

"Hope is a thing with feathers that perches in the Soul and sings the tune without words and never stops... at all."

—Emily Dickinson (1830-1886)

INTRODUCTION

TWO THINGS I WISH THIS BOOK TO DRAW attention to: first, there is a Spiritual Reality and second, that we have a Soul that resides in our body. We are in fact a spiritual entity housed in a human body to participate in the physical world!

My life started out pretty normal in 1946, with two older sisters, a younger sister and an older brother. My parents married in 1940 and divorced in 1949. My first memory was in early 1949. I just turned three years old when I had a Near-Death Experience (NDE). The details will be found in the chapter titled Spiritual Events in Action. My mother found me in a coma one morning soaked in blood. She asked my older sister Sheila to get my father next door. When she returned without my father she told my mom that Dad was in bed with the single mom of two. My mother walked me to the hospital, once I recovered. She then left my dad and divorced him. We lived in Vancouver at the time; she moved us to Victoria in 1949.

She met up with a man soon after we moved to Victoria. He was nine years younger than her; she was only twenty-nine. His name was Bob and he met my older sister at the park by the hotel and she brought him back to the hotel. It did not take long for Mom to fall in love with Bob. He saw an opportunity to have full access to five children. He invited Mom and us to live with him. He then moved us into Navy housing because Bob was in the Navy. He joined up in the months leading up to the Korean War being declared in June 25 1950.

What Mom did not know was that Bob was at the park looking for young girls to molest. He married my mother in 1950. I, my brother, sisters and Mom lived in fear for the next eight years. It started in 1949 and ended in 1957. We all suffered from post-traumatic stress disorder and the complications it produces. Chronic health conditions like addictions, mental health issues, diabetes, etc. However, this book is not about us dealing with those issues, it is about my NDE and other spiritual events throughout my life, including other people I know.

> I read Dr. Eben Alexander's book *Proof of Heaven: A Neurosurgeon's Journey into the Afterlife*, to see what he wrote on the topic. It is only one of many on the subject of NDE, but it's one of my favourites along with *Metaphysics: A Study of Ennead II.1 (40)* by James Wilberding, which examines Plotinus' *Ennead II*. His unions in the higher reality with the 'One' or Absolute Source. "For Plotinus and other Greek mystics his predecessors Plato and Pythagoras, Spirituality means ascent from the lower sense-reality to the higher sense-reality. Greek mystics derived meaning and contemplation of nature. They contemplated the wonder of the invisible spiritual reality, which they saw as the cause and ultimate meaning behind the physical reality."[1]

I have found my answer to my own experiences when I read these stories. Today, more and more of near-death, out of body, and reincarnation experiences are now being recorded. Therefore, it is time to change our worldview on our purpose for being here. Plato had it right when he said:

> *"And of madness there are two kinds; one produced by human infirmity, the other a divine release of the soul from the yoke of custom and convention."*

—Plato (428-347 BC)

The dogma from religion we hold on to is false ideas of creation and why we are here, if there is any reason at all. Today, we need to be more open minded because even science is taking a new look at old ideas of creation more seriously.

There is more and more proof that a Spiritual Reality is a fact, and we do have a Soul. Science is now looking more closely at the stories from people who have experienced some form of spiritual event in their lives that as of yet cannot be explained by science.

My life experiences tell me that religion has only part of the story on creation. You will find that we are truly one in the spirit and have the same DNA as the 'One'. I do not mean physical image of the 'One' because nobody has actually seen the Absolute source, or even describe the physical appearance. Many names have been given but they have described its character traits. Plato called it the 'Good'. Unlike a religious idea of a God, the 'One' does not need to be worshipped; it would be like worshipping yourself. The 'One' made images of itself called the Intellect and Soul with its traits as equals, it wanted other entities to have a personal relationship with, not to be alone anymore.

"Also, there is no hierarchy in this world because we are all one and linked to the Absolute Source of life. A philosophy of Plotinus' combines the mystical with the practical and was to have a great influence on Christian theology. His philosophy is aimed at helping the student to return to have communion with the 'One' or ultimate Being by means of contemplation. As in Christian theology, Plotinus believed in a tripartite of divinities, these being the One, the Intellect, and the Soul. However, unlike the Christian trinity, these are not on an equal footing but rather successive 'stages' or emanations of contemplative being."[2]

I hope this book will open your eyes and lead you to a new worldview of hope rather than a path of fear that only leads to death before your burial. My book is not to prove what to believe in, but only to open a door to finding truth. I know from my own experience that there is a Spiritual Reality and a Soul and in my research I discovered Plotinus' Metaphysics. For the first time intuitively I knew it was true. We, I believe, have come from a Spiritual Reality and are now on a journey that is not that clear to me however, it is unfolding. The 'One's' emanation is still at work but there will be a time we will return to the perfect world – some call Heaven. We all have a right to live our lives on this planet earth without fear of harm in doing so. We are still evolving Souls and need to be less materialistic and try to be more like our higher Soul. It is our purpose to become a God or Love force of acts of love, charity, tolerance, kindness and patience toward our fellow man, other living creatures, and our earth. We can start immortality or wholeness now, why wait?

I liked the idea that we all get to where we need to go to become like the butterfly from a caterpillar; then live in that perfect world again. Why wait for our life to end here before we can enjoy the fruits of heaven? Plotinus knew that all Souls would transform into perfect Souls by the reincarnation process; "One Soul but many bodies". In other words, we will keep coming back until we get it right. The 'One' loves us so the 'One' made it possible for us not to fail! Now that is a loving God. No sin will keep us out of Heaven.

You may ask why there is evil in the world. It is because we have free agency; we can make choices. An urban legend on the Internet attributes a story to Albert Einstein as telling a professor, "God did not create evil. Evil is not like faith or love that exists just like light and heat. Evil is the result of what happens when a man does not have God's love present in his heart. It's like the cold that comes when there is no heat or the darkness that comes when there is no light." Whether or not Einstein actually made such a statement is a moot point, it's still a powerful point. "Things cannot all be good, and indeed, as Plotinus' says, the universe would be less perfect if they were, just as it may be necessary for a beautiful work of art that now all its parts are beautiful in isolation." Plotinus'- listing in the Internet Encyclopedia of philosophy – a good summary of Plotinus' and his teachings.

Creation cannot stop until all emanation from the 'One' has reached all levels of being and imperfection is corrected by our own willpower, before it can be completed. This may take many lifetimes but it will happen. We are only starting the journey of our evolution, but we are moving very fast because our world is now in danger of ending by the works of evil people and governments that oppress the rights of people for power and greed.

PLOTINUS' TEACHINGS IN ROME

THE AGE OF NEO-PLATONISM IS DIRECTLY related to Plotinus' lectures in Rome between 248 AD and 268 AD. His student Porphyry, did all of his recordings from the lectures under the title of *Enneads*. Plotinus' was reworking the philosophy of Plato, and because of Porphyry's close friendship with Plotinus, the subject of the Divine Hypostases and Reincarnation was discussed in detail with his student.

I believe Plotinus' believed he was the reincarnate of Plato and explained his unions with the 'One' with Porphyry. Why else would he be a spiritual-philosophical philosopher if he had not experienced the spiritual union with the 'One'? Those mystical unions he had, made his cosmology more credible than other philosophers. In one of those unions he was told by the 'One' why we were created. Plotinus taught, "The 'One' could not dwell alone but must ever bring forth souls from himself."[3] However, it is not to say others have not had the same experience, it was just not recorded. He came to believe that man should reject material things and then should purify his Soul and gain immortality. The Soul resides in both the spiritual realm and the human conscience and is still one entity with different functions, however, with the same goal. The material world was limited; however the Spiritual Reality is limitless and unchanging in a perfect world.

"The physical emanation came about by a spontaneous operation of nature, designed by the 'One'. Not by the labour of a God per se." When people say, after a disaster or death, how could God let this happen? – the truth is it did not let it happen because it is under the laws of nature in the physical realm, which is becoming more unstable due to our need to control it, something that cannot be controlled at this time. We must learn to protect our environment by living by nature's rules or suffer the consequences. It is karma at work when we abuse nature; it comes back at us in great force.

The Soul, I believe, has the answers to the problems we have on this earth, however we must learn how to access this knowledge so we can intervene. The lower Soul is our human conscious, I believe. Unlike animals, we have human senses as well as human instincts that have a job to do and that is to help us to survive in this physical plain. The higher Soul is more linked to the Spiritual Reality and has access to all knowledge that will lead us in solving our problems. The Soul is one entity but like the human body has different parts, i.e. legs, arms, etc. to function but still one body. Higher and lower does not mean greater, just different functions. It may be the invisible glue that links all information together.

As Deepak Chopra suggests in his article "A Little Boost for Immortality"[4], it is our ego getting us in trouble with our evolution. For example, when a person has a near-death experience, somehow the person opens his heart or mind to the event; then lets it unfold, and trusting his higher power will direct him or her to a satisfactory end. This is called free agency or free choice and the choice is always your Soul's choice but we must decrease the ego so we can hear and see the unseen power at work, and let it work. Socrates said, "The only true wisdom is in knowing you know nothing." [5]

Plotinus' basic teaching to his students was the fact that the 'One' was like us, we need each other, in his union with the Absolute source he was told it no longer wanted to dwell alone and it creates new thoughts as crescent images of itself. The 'One' with its imagination created the Intellect, and the Soul, to have company in its Spiritual Reality. That is why humans and the physical world were created. It is still a mystery to me why humans must evolve, but whatever the reason it is unfolding. We have the same traits, but only in limited amounts, and must allow that higher power to work in our life to get the full benefit or knowledge, that we lack. This problem for the Soul is what Plotinus said: "because Soul, unlike the Intellect, is unable to contemplate the forms immediately, but instead must contemplate them as fragmented objects perceived in moments of succession."

In my view, this is why we get moments of clarity for various reasons, but all come from a higher intelligence. There have been great people throughout our history and in the present day who have demonstrated this great wisdom and power. These people, like their creator, have great ideals and imaginations that they have used to improve mankind and nature. To name a few that helped shape an ideal world in our evolution, because of their ability to love, like a God:

- Moses helped his God to free the Hebrews from slavery.
- Jesus Christ helped his God to free people from the sin of the Soul, another form of slavery.
- Mother Teresa helped her God save thousands of children from starvation, giving them love, shelter and food.
- Dr. Martin Luther King helped his God free his people from injustice and oppression.
- Gandhi helped his higher power in bringing freedom to his people in India.
- Nelson Mandela helped his people to be free from oppression and inequity for all in his country.

PART 1:
PLOTINUS' HYPOSTASIS — HOW THE
PHYSICAL REALITY WAS FORMED

Also central in Plotinus' cosmology is the chain of Hypostasis:

> With regard to the existence that is supremely perfect (i.e. The 'One'), we must say it only produces the very greatest of things that are found below it. But that which after it is the most perfect, the second principle, is intelligence. (Nous) Intelligence contemplates the 'One' and needs nothing but it. But the 'One' has no need of Intelligence (i.e. being the absolute principle, it is totally self sufficient). The 'One' which is superior to intelligence produces Intelligence, which is the best existence as the One, since it is superior to all other beings. The (World) soul is the word (logos) and a phase of the activity of Intelligence just as intelligence is the logos and a phase of the activity of the 'One'. But the logos of the Soul[6] are obscure being only an image of Intelligence. The Soul therefore directs her to intelligence, just as the latter, to be Intelligence, must contemplate the 'One'... Every begotten being longs for the being that begot it and loves it.[7]

THE LOGOS

As the relationship between a Hypostasis and it products, the Logos denotes the plan or formative principle from which the lower realities evolve and by which their development is governed. Plotinus uses the term not to indicate a separate Hypostasis (contra philosophy, Christianity, etc.), but to express the relationship between a Hypostases and its source or its products or both. Plotinus thought this relation between the grades of being, or Hypostasis, is a two-fold process. There is a downward process of Emanation or Out Flowing, and a corresponding upward process to return through Contemplation. This can be represented diagrammatically as follows:

The Divine Hypostasis

The 'One'
The Absolute and Source

▲

Emanation   *Contemplation*

▼

Nous
The 'Divine Mind'

Emanation Contemplation

Psyche

"Soul"; the dynamic, creative temporal power, both cosmic (World-Soul) and individual (e.g. human consciousness) The World of the Senses

PART 2:
PLOTINUS' UNION WITH THE
'ONE' — WHY WE ARE HERE!

Plotinus'

"As one that would draw through the node
of things,
Back sweeping to the vortex of the cone,
Cloistered about with memories, alone
in chaos, while waiting silence sings.

Obliterate *of cycles' wanderings...I was an*
atom on creation's throne
and knew all nothing my unconquered own.
God! Should I be the hand upon the strings?

But I was lonely as a lonely child. I cried amid
the void and heard no cry.
And then for utter loneliness, made I ... New
thoughts as crescent images of
of me. And with them was my essence reconciled...
While fear went forth
from mine eternity."

p.36- collection early poems of
-Ezra Pound (1885-1972)
[Michael King, Ed, 1982]

My understanding of the Cause of Creation is
Plotinus' explains his experience of having a union with
the 'ONE' or Creator, and was told the reason why our
Souls where created,it was because 'It' did not want to
be alone anymore. Very much human I would say!

SPIRITUAL EVENTS IN ACTION

THERE ARE EVENTS THAT I HAVE EXPERIENCED
that could be considered life blessings, miracles and/or
clear understanding of a Spiritual Reality. These events
come when I have a crisis or something out of my
control. I think many of you will relate to these events
and come to realize that life is not what we think it is.
It is my belief we are on a human journey to evolve into
a person that will live in a perfect world; the Soul will
gain wholeness.

NOT A TIME TO DIE

Throughout my life I had a clear memory of me floating outside of my body and viewing my mother coming
down the stairs outside our home in Vancouver. She
was carrying a small child or baby in her arms. It was a
cloudy morning and did not look like a great day to be
going for a walk. I watched with calmness her coming
down the street at a fast walk and then suddenly I am
visiting myself on an operating table with a large over-
head light above me. I must be about three years old.
This memory keeps coming to me over the years and
finally I asked my mother in 1994 of my experience.
She said that one morning when I was three years old,
she found me unconscious and soaked in blood. She had
to carry me to the hospital, which was about ten blocks

from our home, as I lay helpless in her arms. Once she got me to the hospital, the nurses and doctors took me into the operating room and stopped the bleeding and got me breathing again, as I watched from above the operating light. Mother told me I had a bleeding ulcer in my nose and must have bled most of the night and she found me in a comatose state.

Today, this would be called a "near-death experience" and that my soul left my body known as an out of body event that cannot be explained by our current science. The experience seemed like moments or even seconds to me, however, it took my mother at least thirty minutes to get me to the hospital. Still, I was mentally alert and had a sense of calm while my soul was apart from my body.

MIRACLE SAVED DROWNING BOY

In the summer of 1954, I was eight years old. My mother would send her five children to two weeks of summer camps sponsored by the YMCA. My brother and I got to go to the Chief Thunderbird Lake Camp on Vancouver Island near Sooke, British Columbia. We lived near Victoria at the time, out in the country about fifteen miles from Sooke.

The YMCA Chief Thunderbird Lake Park is off the main highway on a winding gravel road with tall fir and pine trees on each side. The road ends by a small lake with a large building and parking area. This large building is the kitchen and main hall and then in front is the lake with a dock and to the west small cabins that house the staff and children. The first night we sat on the beach and roasted hot dogs and drank hot cocoa. There suddenly appeared Indians in their canoes. They were dressed up in their Indian war garments. In the lead canoe was the Chief and they all had bows and arrows. When they shot their arrows, the tips were on fire. The arrows were shooting at a target that had been set up earlier in the day. The arrows looked great flying in the air then hitting the target. We all gathered around the Chief and his braves as they told us stories about their culture. We all loved hearing about their way of life and meeting the Chief and his braves. It was a very exciting night for us children and when we said our goodbyes, it was time for bed.

The first thing in the morning each cabin of children was instructed to run around the small lake, but for an eight-year-old boy it seemed a very long run. We were told before we could eat breakfast we must run around the lake and then go to the kitchen for breakfast. The path around the lake started close to our cabins on the west side. Our cabin housed about ten boys aged eight to ten years old. Once our group got about a third of the way around the lake, another boy, about the same age, and I saw a raft at the lake edge. We could see the dock across the lake close to the main building. It was closer than running around the lake. However, about fifteen feet from the shore the raft started to fall apart. It was not nailed together. A major mistake for me because I could not swim.

The other boy could swim and he got back to shore. I started to drown, slapping my arms and legs in total panic. My third time down in the water I was totally exhausted and underwater in a fetal position, my short life ran before me. Suddenly a beautiful white light entered the lake and seemed to cover me, giving me a sense of calm and reason. I then reached up and grabbed a log from the raft and pulled myself up to get air. I paddled, my arms still holding onto the log and reached the shore. I noticed right away the sun was shining brightly on the other side of the lake. The white light that covered me was an Angel I believed at the time. This was in fact a spiritual intervention to save my life. I believe it was a miracle. The boys that were with me were nowhere in sight. None of the boys tried to help me out of the water, I thought later on in life. This was a near-death experience because I would have drowned for sure! I guess it was not my time to die.

Doug Zeigler

AN ANGEL IN THE PARKING LOT

After a long trip back from a Christmas and New Year's holiday on January 2, 1991, I returned to work the next day. By the end of the day I was very sick from a chest cold. I had dinner and laid down for an hour, when I woke I decided to get some cold medication. I got to the drug store about 7:45 p.m.; closing was 8:00 p.m. so I was in and out of the store. When I sat down in my car I had a serious chest pain – I knew I was in trouble because I had my first heart attack in 1988 at age forty-two. I decided to calm myself and wait for a car to pull into the drug store parking lot. Just as I thought that, a car pulled up beside me, we were the only cars in the lot.

I opened my car door and said to the woman getting out of her car that I needed help because I was having a heart attack. She was taken back because it was dark outside and not much lighting. She said "how do you know?" I then tried to answer but threw up beside my car door. She then realized I was telling the truth and said to me she was a registered nurse and would get help in the drug store and be right back. She came back right away with the Pharmacist. They gave me medication for the chest pain. The EMS showed up and took me to the hospital.

I was having a heart attack and the cause was due to water on my lungs. I had a mild heart attack and was in hospital for three weeks and off work for three months for heart rehabilitation. I know the RN was not an angel or was she? Another spiritual intervention in my life, and I know if this woman did not show up at that moment, I would have died without immediate treatment, which I received with the quick action. I never got to thank her or the staff at the store in Edmonton but my prayers are that I wish them all the best in their lives, good health and happiness.

A DREAM INTERVENTION

In 1971, I became a Type 1 or insulin dependent diabetic; I was only twenty-five years old. It has caused many problems for me with diabetes complications. The management of the disease has improved over those forty-two years because of better insulin and glucose blood monitors. However, because we do not live in a glass tube we will experience low and high blood glucose levels from time to time. When your blood glucose levels are high, you will take fast-acting insulin to bring it into a normal range, likewise when it is too low you must take sugar to get it into normal range. Both situations are serious and if not acted on you will die. I have had many highs and lows over the years but have been very lucky in recognizing the symptoms of both – then treating the problem. Normal range for glucose levels are between 4 and 6.

In April 2013, I had a dream that actually saved my life I believe. I was dreaming I was walking with a friend; we were on our way to have lunch. One of the symptoms is feeling hungry, which I did, but it would be about an hour before we could eat. Out of the blue, we were passing a picnic table with two men in white suits. I thought to myself – how strange – then one of the men said, "you must eat now, do not wait!"

So I forced myself out of a dead sleep and knew I was seriously low, so I checked to make sure. It was 1.8 – remember I said normal range was 4 to 6. If I had waited for lunch I would have gone into diabetic shock and gone into a coma or died. With my heart condition most likely I would have died. The men in white suits were Angels I believe, their mission was to awaken me, because the blood sugar was too low for me to detect in a deep sleep and to treat with my bedside sugar tabs. Also, I could not identify the man walking with me to go for lunch, but all he talked about was eating. Again, I know that someone is looking out for me and I do not debate when I get a message. I act and trust it is important for me to act on the message because it is for my well-being.

SPIRITUAL EVENTS BY OTHERS

A MOMENT OF CLARITY — BY
JOHN BATT JR. (PEN NAME)

MY ALCOHOLISM STARTED AT THE AGE OF sixteen and ended when I was thirty-five years old. It was November 16, 1981 when I went to an AA meeting and had a "Moment of Clarity". The event seemed like time stood still. I seemed to be in another place and alone, for the first time I accepted that I was an alcoholic. A voice told me I needed to stay at the meeting to recover from my addiction. I did not know at the time the desire to drink was removed from me. Actually, there were at least twenty people at that meeting and we were midway through the meeting – I had this moment of clarity or miracle. Believe me, I tried everything to stop abusing myself from drinking. I was at the state of my addiction called Stage 3 – exhaustion, death was just around the corner if I could not quit somehow. I do not wish to focus on my drinking career and all the suffering it caused me and others, but the spiritual intervention that took place.

The moment of clarity has been recorded by many alcoholics, and they were blessed with a freedom from their addiction to alcohol. However, this disease needed more than a miracle to keep them sober, many others say it took a few years to overcome the compulsion to use, which AA calls an educational kind of experience. Also, most people need a support group to stay sober or clean. All diseases have symptoms; alcoholism is really not the correct name for this disease. In the 1930's, Dr. Silkworth gave it the name because most if not all his patients used this substance to feed their addiction. He had it right when he described it as a psychological and physical condition. However, a more recent term is called Addictive Personality Syndrome (APS).[8]

In 1935, Alcoholics Anonymous was formed and served very well in helping people maintain sobriety under their 12-step program. The movement has grown into the millions and also created other 12 step programs to help people with other addictions like gambling, and drugs etc. However, because the program was built on the idea of a spiritual solution, due to Bill Wilson's 'Spiritual Awakening', however for him to recover from his unmanageable life he needed a support group. Six months after his deliverance from his addiction, he needed to talk to another alcoholic while on a sales trip. Where he got this idea, in my opinion was a spiritual event; it came to him in a hotel, and instead of going back drinking he phoned a hospital to find out who was a drunk like himself. This is how he met the co-founder of AA, Dr. Bob. The AA movement needed 'talk therapy' to help people to gain full recovery. Later, Dr. Durand F. Jacobs provided a modern idea of the disease and has shown through his research that the symptoms are the same for all addictive behaviors, therefore it does not matter what substance or activity the addict takes or does, it will bring on the symptoms. Dissociative-like reactions experienced by addicts or APS subjects can experience: Trance, Different person, Outside self, and Blackouts. The addict loses track of time.

AA must really look at the reasons for its success so it will not die. It is my understanding that social research has established that people who join a group with the same purpose or goal are much more success-ful in maintaining better health, no matter what disease it is. Also a 12-step program is very therapeutic in changing negative lifestyles into a more productive way of life. Saying all this does not take away why some of us experienced a moment of clarity or having a spiritual awakening that released us from compulsive drinking, and others needed the AA program to find recovery from their addiction(s). For me, my last days of drink-ing were a living hell; suicide seemed to be the only way out. I wondered many times why I had a problem with addictions. I blamed my upbringing; it provided predisposing psychological conditions that needed treatment. Taking on the role of being a victim allowed me not to take any responsibility for my disease. Then one day I realized it had nothing to do with my life cir-cumstances, it was a disease and it needed treatment. I found a support program helpful in my life. Somehow I went into the unseen world and found the grace of a higher power to restore me to sanity and a 'talk therapy' support group to keep me in recovery. After thirty-two years of sobriety, I realized my disease is an addiction, alcohol provided the high I chased until my near death.

A SPIRITUAL AWAKENING — BY
BILL WILSON (1900-1971)

My depression deepened unbearably and finally it seemed to me as though I were at the bottom of the pit. I still gagged badly on the notion of a Power greater than myself, but finally, just for the moment, the last vestige of my proud obstinacy was crushed. All at once I found myself crying out, "If there is a God, let Him show Himself! I am ready to do anything, anything!"

Suddenly the room lit up with a great white light. I was caught up into ecstasy which there is not words to describe. It seemed to me, in the mind's eye, that I was on a mountain and that a wind not of air but of spirit was blowing and then it burst upon me that I was a free man. Slowly the ecstasy subsided. I lay on the bed, but now for a time I was in another world, a new world of consciousness. All about me and through me there was a wonderful feeling of Presence, and I thought to myself, "So this is God of the preachers! A great peace stole over me and I thought, 'No matter how wrong things seem to be, they are still all right. Things are all right with God and His world.'"[9]

Bill Wilson's account of his profound Spiritual Awakening. Wilson was the co-founder of Alcoholics Anonymous. His description of this event is on the Internet and in a movie on his life and in the A.A. Big Book.

RICHARD'S PREMONITION (PEN NAME)

This is a true event that occurred to a friend, which he believed saved his life. Richard had a premonition on his way home. He was returning from a holiday on a red-eye flight. It was exhausting because he could not sleep on the plane. He arrived at Calgary International Airport late that night, got his truck from the parking lot, and left for home which was 175 miles south of Calgary.

Just outside a town called Bassano, he had a premonition of falling asleep at the wheel and rolling his pick-up truck and landing upside down in a ditch alongside the highway. This thought and picture of a possible accident made him stop at Bassano Truck Stop. He rested for about half an hour and had a coffee. He felt refreshed and he now started again on his trip home.

He got about twelve miles south of Bassano when he came across an accident. The EMS had just arrived as well. There was a pick-up truck rolled over resting on its roof. Richard, the EMS, and a RCMP officer pulled out a young man from the truck. He died at the scene. Richard later found out he was only thirty-seven years old, also from Medicine Hat. Richard was reading an article in the paper a few days later about the accident, the police believed the victim went to sleep at the wheel, because there was no other cause, drinking was ruled out.

He was very happy he listened to his premonition and took a break from driving because prior to his break, he also nearly fell asleep. He now thinks there is a higher power that provides us with premonitions to change our course of action or be more prepared for the unexpected. In his case, once he had this thought and a picture of the accident, he stopped to take a rest from driving and have a coffee to help him stay awake. He thinks this accident could have been him. He now listens more closely to his premonitions and intuitions. He now trusts that these messages are from a God of his understanding and must act on the message.

ED FAHL'S NDE — BY SHELLEY LABELLE (DAUGHTER)

In 1995, my dad had a blood clot in his leg. The doctor admitted him to the hospital in Kamloops, B.C. and the doctor on duty gave him an experimental drug – it was a blood thinner to dissolve the blood clot.

However, he had a reaction to the drug. Due to the reaction, he went into cardiac arrest. The doctors told us his heart stopped for a whole four minutes, however they brought him back, then put him in ICU. The family gathered at the ICU and we were allowed to visit one at a time.

I was the first sibling to see Dad. After a few minutes I asked him if he saw a light when his heart stopped. He said he would tell me later; however my sister Annette asked him again when she was with him because she was worried he might die before he could tell us. He told her yes he did but will give the details later. When he got home from the hospital he then told us what happened and Dad was always honest so we had no doubt about what he said was true. First Dad got choked up with tears running down his face when he started telling us of his amazing experience. He said he was in great pain when he lost consciousness; his heart had stopped for four minutes the doctor told him later. He heard a loud scream and then found himself in a dark tunnel, his first reaction was where is my rifle, and being a hunter and former soldier his fear took over.

He then turned around this bend in the tunnel and saw a very warm bright light. He immediately felt calm, at peace, and had no more pain. He looked up at the light and saw two young women standing there. As he got closer he realized it was his sister Johanna who passed away ten years earlier and his mother who died when he was seventeen years old. He was so happy seeing them he tried to get closer, however they waved their arms, pointing for him to go back. He really wanted to stay, but the next thing he was back on the operating table in a lot of pain. We told Dad he should sue the doctor for his mistake in giving him the drug that caused his heart attack. However, Dad said he should thank the doctor because he got to see his mother and sister and he now knew there was a heaven. He cried because he wanted to be with his mother and sister, however his wife needed him more.

I think that is why he did not die, to continue to help our mother Sheila. He lived another seventeen years after his NDE and died in 2011. Sheila, his wife of forty-three years died before him in 2004. He looked after her very well as she had many chronic health problems. Because of Dad she spent her time at home, not in a nursing home. My father was very lonely after Mom passed. Then, he met Ola, my husband's mother. She came out to visit from her home in Ontario for our daughter's graduation. She was now single, being divorced for a number of years.

My Dad and Ola became friends and they decided to live together to share their interests and company, and were together until his passing. He died from a heart attack on his way home from a dinner at my home. His oldest daughter Annette came out from her home in Alberta for a surprise visit and we all had a dinner together. After dinner, Dad said he wanted to go home as he was not feeling well. The family was thrilled for both of them when they moved in together because they enjoyed many things together and both Dad and Ola were not alone anymore. After our father's passing, my mother-in-law now lives with me and her son Lloyd, my husband. All of us children are very grateful knowing there is life after death and we will see our parents and family when it is time for us to depart from this world.

ASTRAL TRAVEL: A TRUE STORY — BY GERRI ARUNDELL

Early 1970, I had a great experience. I was pregnant at the time with my daughter Tanya. My husband Rod and I had just finished dinner. I went for a sleep feeling tired and fell asleep very quickly. Still asleep, I found myself floating above my body on the bed. I felt very good but a little frightened. Then to my amazement, I floated out into the living room where my husband was watching TV. He was laughing and I was calling his name to get his attention, however with no luck.

I then realized he could not hear me so I went to the front door and wanted to leave but was afraid I might not be able to get back in. I felt very good and had a sense of freedom that I had never had before and wanted to float more. I sensed I should return to my bedroom and then returned to my body still sleeping on the bed. When I woke I felt exhausted. I went rushing to tell my husband in the living room. He was still watching TV. He looked up at me while I told him what happened. He said in a calm voice that he had heard similar stories before and did not doubt my experience at all.

A few years later my girlfriend asked me if I had ever Astral Traveled before. This was the first person I had told other than my husband. However, I did not know the term Astral Travel, she explained it to me and told me of her experiences. She said that she had had many out of body trips, some to ancient countries. I said, "ancient countries?" Yes, she said, not only out of body, but memories of past lives in ancient places she lived. She also added she had no fear of not returning to her body and enjoyed these events. When it first happened, I was afraid to tell anybody, now people talk about them as if they were an every day event. We hear about these events from recent books on the subject, especially about NDEs.

My experience has given me hope of life after death and when Doug sent us an essay he wrote on the 'One' and Immortality, he said he was going to turn it into a book. I shared my experience with him and he requested that I send him my story – he would then add it to his book. We hope it becomes a reality for Doug because he believes these events like many others today are worthwhile to study. I hope my story helps to this end.

PHIL ISAACSON'S NDE

It was February, 1968. I was living in Vancouver at the time of my NDE, this is what I recall. I was suffering from severe depression and I found myself in a dark state of depression, in fact suicidal. In planning my suicide I did not want my loved ones to know I took my own life. I came up with the idea of finding out how to discover the source of the electric part of my existence. Once I found it I believed I could simply turn it off and I would appear to have died in my sleep.

I sprawled backwards, spread eagled on my bed. I remember feeling all my emotions pouring out of me at a high speed. Myriad vibrations from my entire life were just rushing out. Then I was empty. I went into my head to search for the off switch. I was inside total darkness. My search grew frantic. I was aware of a physical limit to this dark sort of conscience. The outer limit of it was curved. In desperation I tried to break out. I was a small point racing along dragging sparks as I tried to cut my way out of this black curved limitation above me. As if my Soul was screaming for release.

I suddenly broke through and this vast great dark prison instantly dwindled down to nothing as I flew above and beyond it. Above and beyond into a dimension of light and geometric patterns and colours. I had no body and I was soaring through it all in such a state of joy. There was also a sound that was not really music but so absolutely beautiful. There was something more important than the beauty of the sound and light. I was also receiving from outside myself, the knowledge that I was experiencing what was to come in its own time. This was not my voice I was hearing. It was not my own thought. The knowledge came outside of me. Along with knowing that after this life something unimaginably beautiful would happen, I was basically let known that no matter how unendurable life on earth may seem, it's small stuff in the big picture. Do not sweat the small stuff. The next thing I remembered was my eyes opened. I was blank. Did not know who or what I was. A nerve twitched and made me realize I was seeing my forearms. I was in a fetal position and it was as if I had just popped out of my body. I was back.

I do not know how much time elapsed during this experience, an instant or an hour? I have carried my belief in a greater existence after death since that time. I only wish I could describe the light, colour, music, or sound. It was like a heavenly, harmonic tone. The knowledge given to me was given in a reassuring, loving way. I cannot describe it any better than this unfortunately.

Adios, may the Force be with you.

Phil

A DREAM OF COMFORT — BY SHELLEY LABELLE

My father passed away two months prior to my dream. I was diagnosed with cancer and needed to have an operation to remove it. My father, mother, and husband were always my rock, now faced with this fear, I did not know what to do because my daughters were both grown but they are very close to us emotionally. I did not want them to fear this situation so I put on a brave face in front of them. However, I was very scared. A week before my operation I had a dream – my father came to me. We sat at the dining room table and discussed many things. Before he left me he said I was going to be okay, he assured me not to worry. My father and mother were always there for us children. After this dream I knew in my heart that dad was right and my fear went away.

A DREAM TO SHOW WHAT IS IMPORTANT IN LIFE — BY NETTIE FAHL

I was very busy in our lives, my husband and me. Also our son lives with us. All of us work, and living in

Hinton, near Jasper, Alberta is very far from my sister, brothers and parents. I had a terrible dream that a good friend and family member were going to die. The names were not given to me, who was going to die, and I was confused on the meaning of the dream. Nine days later a good friend died from a heart attack, he was only forty-two years old. We had not seen him and his wife for a while and I felt guilty we did not take the time to visit them. Close to a year after my dream, my brother Danny, also forty-two years old, died from a massive heart attack.

Now I realize we cannot take things for granted and we need to take the time to talk or visit our family and friends. I believe my dream was a wake-up call on what is really important in life, and that is our family and friends. Please do not dismiss a dream, it may have a message for you, not to say you can change the outcome, but at least it may give you an idea of the importance for you.

THE PROOF IS IN THE PUDDING

THERE ARE MORE AND MORE RECORDINGS OF near-death, out of body and reincarnation events each day. Just go on the Internet, or read books by spiritual leaders and scientists. For example, the recent discovery of the Higgs Boson or the God particle is a sub-atomic particle in collision between two protons, it decays almost immediately into two jets of hadrons and two electrons visible as lines. This is the Big Bang I believe that seems to have created the universe and all its entities. Cosmic treacle spread through the universe creating life forms, as Plotinus' emanation process is light or life waves, spreading out through space.

I think Higgs Boson and the Emanation are one and the same. I also believe it was the 'One' that made this event happen for its own purpose, maybe to reflect its internal activities by the way of entities like the Intellect, and Soul. The Soul is the image of the 'One', and the Soul has all the gifts of its creator; no limitations, unlike humans, it only has limited abilities that came about by a spontaneous operation of nature. In its evolution or constant change are the biological instincts, our biological instincts and human senses to help with our survival. Not until we see our true nature can we benefit from our full potential. Our Soul has no limits and resides in the Spiritual Reality and the lower part of the Soul is our intuitive nature in the Physical Reality. Plotinus was a spiritual master like Christ, he could visit and have union with the Divine and I believe we can too, by meditation or intent to do so. I think humans are on a journey to be reunited with their spiritual self to gain wholeness. Deepak Chopra states "immortality is just a synonym for wholeness."[10]

I think there are many ways that people have discovered their true self, may it be a near-death experience, an out of body experience, a memory of a reincarnation(s) or past life, a spiritual awakening and/or even religion. However, it comes down to choice, to hang on to the false reality, or mirror the Good of the Divine to the world. Boethius (AD 480-524) said "those who obtain divinity become Gods... but by nature there is only one God but many by participation."[11] Your Soul will become a 'God' or 'Love' once you decide this is your course of action and this is why some Souls have powers over the physics of this world.

The Creator has provided ways to speak to your heart. By the lower Soul or intuitive ability or by having supernatural cosmic events come about. Here are some examples:

- Intuition – the power of knowing things without conscious reasoning.
- Dreams – bring wisdom inspiration and visions.
- Premonition – have a warning and when the premonition occurs change your course of action.
- Astral Travel – your soul leaves your body and visits places of interest or past lives.
- NDE – you seemed to have died and you may find yourself out of your body and in a tunnel, then a bright light appears, it may transport you to another place, like heaven or just return you to your body or both.
- A Spiritual Awakening – brings freedom from your addictions or other health problems
- A Moment of Clarity – brings a clear message of wisdom for you to act on; you will receive a miracle and have the power to change negative behaviour.

- Clairvoyant – you may see behind the Veil
  and see loved ones who have passed on
  or be given knowledge on a subject beyond your education or training.

When you are in that experience of a spiritual event you will feel some or all of these things. In that moment it seems that time stands still, you will be calm and able to reason, you will know a peace that is beyond descrip-tion, feel a love you never experienced before and you will feel that everything will be okay.

MYSTICAL EVENTS AND WISDOM QUOTES

AND POEMS OF INSPIRATION

THESE ARE QUOTES FROM PEOPLE WHO HAVE seen the mystical Spiritual Reality and some of their wisdom in leading to positive change.

Dr. Eben Alexander in his book, *Proof of Heaven*, states from his near-death experience that while in the Core, he was given these messages by what he called OM:

1. "You are loved and cherished dearly and forever."

2. "You have nothing to fear."

3. "There is nothing you can do wrong."

Plotinus had an out of body experience with what he called the 'One'. "Often I have woken to myself out of body, become detached from all else and entered into myself and I have seen beauty of surpassing greatness and have felt assured that then especially I belonged to the higher reality and identified with the Divine."[12]

Don Miguel Ruiz wrote *The Four Agreements: A Practical Guide to Personal Freedom* (A Toltec Wisdom Book). The story is about a Toltec man studying to be a medicine man, around three thousand years ago. He had an experience he described as:

> "One day as he slept in a cave, he dreamed that he saw his own body sleeping. He came out of the cave on the night of a new moon. The sky was clear, and he could see millions of stars. Then something happened inside of him that transformed his life forever. He looked at his hands, he felt his body, and heard his own voice saying 'I am made of light, and I am made of stars.' He looked at the stars again and realized that it is not the stars that create light but rather light that creates the stars. Everything is made of light, he said and the space in between is not empty. And he knew that everything that exists is one living being, and that light is the messenger of life, because it is alive and contains all information. Then he realized that although he was made of stars, he was not those stars. *I am in between the stars,* he thought. So he called the stars the tonal and the light between the stars the nagual, and he knew that what created the harmony and space between the two is life or intent. Without life the tonal and nagual could not exist. Life is the force of the absolute, the supreme, the creator who creates everything. This is what he discovered; everything in existence is

manifestation of a living being we call God. Everything is God."[13]

THE FOUR AGREEMENTS: A PRACTICAL GUIDE TO PERSONAL FREEDOM (A TOLTEC WISDOM BOOK)

4. Be impeccable with your word:
   Speak with integrity. Say only what you mean. Avoid using the word against yourself or gossip about others. Use the power of your word in the direction of truth and love.

5. Do not take anything personally:
   Nothing others do is because of you. What others say or do is a projection of their reality, their own dream. When you are immune to the opinions of others and actions of others, you will not be the victim of needless suffering.

6. Do not make assumptions:
   Find the courage to ask questions and express what you really want. Communicate with others as clearly as you can to avoid misunderstandings, sadness, and drama. With just this one agreement, you can completely transform your life.

7. Always do your best:
   Your best is going to change moment to moment; it will be different when you are healthy as opposed to sick. Under any circumstances, simply do your best and you will avoid self-judgment, self-abuse, and regret.

—Don Miguel Ruiz

Doug Zeigler

Tao Te Ching Words of Wisdom
(The Way of Life)

Live and let live.
Do not judge.
Take it as it comes.
Everything will be okay.

—Lao Tzu (500 BC)

Wisdom of Buddha

I calm my breathing, I relax my body, and I observe my
thoughts with detachment.
I observe the environment around me.
I am aware of the precariousness of each living thing.
I free myself of every attachment.
I let my love for all beings grow.

Gililio Cesare Giacobbe
(How to Become a Buddha in 5 Weeks)

Desiderata (1927)

Go placidly amid the noise and haste, and remember
what peace there may be in silence. As far as possible
without surrender be on good terms with all persons.
Speak your truth quietly and clearly; and listen to others,
even the dull and ignorant; they too have their story.

Avoid loud and aggressive persons; they are vexa-
tions to the spirit. If you compare yourself with others,
you may become vain and bitter; for always there will
be greater and lesser persons than yourself.

Enjoy your achievements as well as your plans. Keep
interested in your career, however humble; it is a real
possession in the changing fortunes of time. Exercise

caution in your business affairs; for the world is full of trickery. But let this not blind you to what virtue there is; many persons strive for high ideals. And everywhere life is full of heroism. Be yourself. Especially, do not feign affection. Neither be critical about love; for in the face of all aridity and disenchantment it is as perennial as the grass.

Take kindly the counsel of the years, gracefully surrendering the things of youth. Nurture strength of the spirit to shield you in sudden misfortune. But do not distress yourself with imaginings. Many fears are born of fatigue and loneliness.

Beyond a wholesome discipline, be gentle with yourself. You are a child of the universe, no less than the trees and the stars; you have a right to be here. And whether or not it is clear to you, no doubt the universe is unfolding as it should. Therefore be at peace with God, whatever you conceive Him to be; and what labors and aspirations, in a noisy confusion of life keep peace with your soul. With all its sham, drudgery and broken dreams, it is still a beautiful world. Be careful. Strive to be happy."

—Max Ehrmann (1872-1945)

CHILD ABUSE

"When a child is harmed by evil, evil will conquer his Soul, but once touched by Love, evil can no longer grow!"

—*Doug Zeigler*

THERE IS TIME

There is time to enjoy the marvels of life, if you take one day at a time. Making each step a simple path to follow and allowing humour into our souls...

To procrastinate is to stay stagnant...T o hurry is to miss the flowers bloom; but to live in the moment we will have control to live each day to its fullest and allow us to have joy, instead of sorrow;

Therefore plan, and organize your activities as if it was your last day. Fate may interrupt this day so be flexible with an alternative plan.

Remember, success comes from action toward your purpose in achieving your goal... so to reach that goal, you must picture it and continue to dream it!

Do not let negativity enter your mind or soul...you will be dead before your time, even before your burial!

Remember awareness of self allows you from being a product of society, and frees you to be you.

Remember love of self integrates you with the universe that wills you to be loved unconditionally for eternity.

Remember time is man-made to schedule business, however, your time is eternal.

Remember to risk being successful and you will be, by giving it your best go!

Remember to look to God for help and He will do so; and in His time we will discover the mysteries of life."

—Doug Zeigler

PRAYER OF ST. FRANCIS

Lord make me the instrument of Your peace

Where there is hatred... Let me sow Love

Where there is injury... pardon

Where there is doubt... faith

Where there is despair... hope

Where there is darkness... light

And where there is sadness... joy

The Proof is in the Pudding

O Divine Master, grant that

I may not seek

To be consoled as... to console

To be understood... as to understand

To be loved... as to love

For

It is in giving... that we receive

It is in pardoning... that we are pardoned

It is in dying... that we are born to eternal life

—St. Francis of Assisi (1182-1226)

SUCCESS

Success is not something to wait
for, it's something to work for.

Achievement...a time for looking back
with pride, for looking ahead with joy.

The talent of success is nothing more
than doing what you can do well

and doing well whatever you do without thought
of fame. If it comes at all it will come because it
is deserved, not because it is sought after.

—Henry Wadsworth Longfellow
(Poet and Educator) (1807-1882)

Eyes

Your eyes are an open book... But only for me to read, God has allowed me to see the beauty; not the outer beauty, but your inner true perfection!

—Doug Zeigler

SUMMARY

I WROTE ARTICLES ON MY NDE EXPERIENCES in 1995 for the *Calgary Herald* for its Christmas Stories on Miracles; Religion Section "Miracle Saved Drowning Boy" and again in 2010 an article called "I'm a Spiritual Being having a Human Being Experience", under my pen name for *The Violet Ray*, Natural Health and Conscious Living Digest.[15]

In that article, I gave four stories based on true accounts of spiritual events I had. In January 2013, I was driven to write more on the subject, due to an article I read on the Internet in 2011 about Plotinus' cosmology and more importantly his unions with the Creator of the universe, which gave me more insight on my personal experiences than any other.

This book started a long time ago when I asked my mother in 1994 about my NDE at age three. In other words, it did not start recently because of current books out on the market. I have written three essays since January 2013, trying to get a story based on true events to write this book. I was driven to write this book by some unknown force or intelligence. I could not sleep, I woke in the middle of the night with ideas that I had never had before.

Many came from research about Plotinus' cosmology. In fact, I went to the public library one day in March 2013, after my first essay. That day by chance, there was a book sale at the library. I was drawn to the books of poetry; the first book of poetry I picked up was a book by the poet Ezra Pound, which I purchased. The second page was page 36, and before my eyes was Plotinus' one of his unions with the 'One', giving his description of an event he had. That sonnet gave me the reason why we were here.

In my first essay I had Part 1: The how the physical world was created, but I did not have the reason why we were created, now I did; so I added this to the second essay under Part 2.

About the same time I was getting a rental movie from the store, I requested "The Notebook", however the sales clerk gave me a movie call "The Impossible". I took the movie home and discovered it was the wrong movie but I decided to watch it anyway. It was about a family of five, two parents and three sons. They were on holidays in Thailand in 2004, at the time of the Tsunami. The mother had a NDE; she had drowned and then was brought back to life. It showed her at the bottom of the water then a beautiful light entered the water and took her up to get air. She then grabbed on to something and heard her oldest son crying for her. They both got to higher ground and were saved. Her husband was separated from them, however managed to get their younger boys to high ground. This memory came back to her when she was being operated on at the makeshift hospital for the victims of the flooding caused by the tsunami. Here again I find it no coincidence of getting this movie, it was no accident, the reason I believe was to provide support in writing this book. There are no coincidences in my life anymore. There is a reason for everything. We must learn to listen to that inner voice and rely on a higher power to guide us.

It pays off when you get rid of your ego. Things happen when you seek help from a higher power and I must say good things. I decided to follow the Toltec Four Agreements to complete my transition from my negative thinking into positive living. It also helps in gaining wisdom from the higher Soul. This in itself is a miracle; I now refuse to be a victim of life circumstances.

The end result is my personal freedom to be me, to enjoy my humanness and to live in the moment! I believe Plotinus was not happy with the human condition and this is why he purified his mind and soul to have a union with the 'One' to find happiness. We can as well, before we die, by our intent to meet our maker. This would give us hope for a better life in the Spiritual Reality, than the suffering we have in the physical reality. His communion quoted earlier expresses this: "and I have seen beauty of surpassing greatness and felt assured that especially I belonged to the higher reality and identified with the Divine."[16] He knew that at the end of his life he would be in that higher reality. What a gift to us knowing we will be there too. As many others who have been there, and have come back from their NDE to tell us. Our world is also beautiful, and we should try to make it better by looking after it more and each other by being a Beacon of Love to the world.

READING LIST AND MOVIES
ON THE SUBJECT:

BOOKS

Alexander, Eben (2012) *Proof of Heaven: A Neurosurgeon's Journey into the Afterlife.* New York: Simon & Schuster.

Chopra, Deepak (2010). "A Little Boost for Immortality" in *The Violet Ray Natural Health and Conscious Living Digest, Spring 2010* (online only)

Dyer, Wayne (2012) *Wishes Fulfilled: Mastering the Art of Manifesting.* New York: Hay House Inc. (Also a 6 CD set available at www.drwaynedyer.com/products/catalog/3631.)

Gordon, Nadine (2009) *The Rose Path.* Raleigh, NC: Lulu.

McPeake, J. D. (2012). *William D. Silkworth, M.D., and the origin and development of Alcoholics Anonymous (A.A.).* Dublin NH, 03444: The Dublin Group, Inc.

Plotinus (1952). *The Enneads.* (Stephen MacKenna and B.S. Page, Tr.) New York: Encyclopedia Brittanica (Ist. Ed.)

Piper, Don and Murphey, Cecil. (2004) *90 Minutes in Heaven – A True story of death and life.* Ada, MI: Baker Publishing Group.

Plotinus (1950). *The Philosophy of Plotinus* (Sterling Lamprecht, Ed.) New York: Appleton-Century Crofts Inc.

Pound, Ezra (1982). *The Collected Early Works of Ezra Pound*, (Michael King, Ed.)

Ruiz, Don Miguel Ruiz (1997). *The Four Agreements: A Practical Guide to Personal Freedom* (A Toltec Wisdom Book)

Stockl, Albert (1887). *Pre-Scholastic Philosophy.* Dublin: M. H. Gill and Son.

Stokes, Philip. (2012) *Philosophy: 100 Essential Thinkers*

Walsch, Neale Donald (2002). *Conversations with God: An Uncommon Dialogue.* New York: Putnum Adult. See also his other books and his movie on his experience talking with God.

Zukav, Gary (2007), *The Seat of the Soul.* New York: Simon & Schuster.

MOVIES

Belon, Maria (2012). *The Impossible.* Director J. A. Bayona. Ocscar-nominated and award-winning story of a tourist family in Thailand caught in the destruction and chaotic aftermath of the 2004 Indian Ocean tsunami. The mother has a NDE by drowning.

(2005) *What the Bleep!?: Down the Rabbit Hole.* Directed by William Arntz, Betsy Chasse and Mark Vicente. Interviews with scientists and authors, animated bits, and a storyline involving a deaf photographer are used in this docudrama to illustrate the link between quantum mechanics, neurobiology, human consciousness and day-to-day reality.

(ENDNOTES)

1. Freedom and Grace Forum: http://freedomandgrace.com/index.php?topic=8462.0;wap2. Accessed 16 April 2014.

2. Stokes, Philip. (2012) Philosophy: 100 Essential Thinkers, page 75.

3. Pound, Ezra (1982). The Collected Early Works of Ezra Pound, (Michael King, Ed.) p 296.

4. Chopra, Deepak. "A Little Boost for Immortality" in Huffington Post, May 4, 2010. Accessed at www.huffingtonpost.com/deepak-chopra/a-little-boost-for-immort_b_525989.html. Accessed 16 April 2014.

5. http://en.wikiquote.org/wiki/Socrates. Accessed 18 April 2014.

6. Soul: the dynamic, creative temporal power, both cosmic ("World Soul") and individual (i.e. human consciousness). From The Internet Encyclopedia of Philosophy; a peer-reviewed resource with a good summary of Plotinus and his teachings. Accessed at www.iep.utm.edu/plotinus/. Accessed on 16 April 2014.

7. Plotinus (1950). The Philosophy of Plotinus (Sterling Lamprecht, Ed.), Chapter 16.

8. Established by Dr. Durand F. Jacobs, PhD., ABPP, Clinical Professor of Medicine (Psychology), Loma Linda University Medical School, California.

9. McPeake, J. D. (2012). William D. Silkworth, M.D., and the origin and development of Alcoholics Anonymous (A.A.). Dublin NH: The Dublin Group, Inc. Accessed at www.dubgrp.com/original_articles. Accessed 16 April 2014.

10. 0 Chopra, Deepak. "A Little Boost for Immortality" in Huffington Post, May 4, 2010. Accessed at www.huffingtonpost.com/deepak-chopra/a-little-boost-for-immort_b_525989.html. Accessed 18 April 2014.

11. 1 Stokes, Philip. (2012) Philosophy: 100 Essential Thinkers, page 82.

12. 2 Plotinus. The Enneads, iv 8. Accessed at www.pantheism.net/paul/history/plotinus.htm. Accessed on 16 April 2014

13. 3 Ruiz, Don Miguel Ruiz (1997). The Four Agreements: A Practical Guide to Personal Freedom (A Toltec Wisdom Book) pages xiii-xiv.

14. 4 Stockl, Albert (1887). Pre-Scholastic Philosophy. Accessed at www3.nd.edu/Departments/Maritain/etext/hhp52.htm. Accessed on 16 April 2014.

15. 5 The Violet Ray. Accessed at www.thevioletray.ca/distribution.html. Accessed 16 April 2014.

16. 6 Plotinus. Enneads iv 8.Doug Zeigler

Doug Zeigler

Printed in Canada